A COMPANY GUIDE TO COMPLETING A RESIDENTIAL UNIT FOR MOVE IN

James B Pratt Jr
A Company Guide To Completing A Residential Unit For Move in

All rights reserved
Copyright © 2023 by James B Pratt Jr

No part of this publication may be reproduced, distributed, or transmitted in any form or by any means, including photocopying, recording, or other electronic or mechanical methods, without the prior written permission of the publisher, except in the case of brief quotations embodied in critical reviews and certain other noncommercial uses permitted by copyright law.

Published by BooxAi
ISBN: 978-965-578-445-9

A COMPANY GUIDE TO COMPLETING A RESIDENTIAL UNIT FOR MOVE IN

JAMES B PRATT JR

CONTENTS

INTRODUCTION

Making a unit market-ready can be challenging for maintenance technicians and contractors. This can become difficult for technicians who are completing unit turns in-house. Calculating the technician's normal job duties, work orders, and time will become an obstacle when making any unit market ready for move in. With over 15 years of experience with unit turns, I have created the perfect guide for companies, contractors, and maintenance technicians to follow to complete units promptly with top-tier quality. This short guide will offer solutions, techniques, and a few trade tricks to help you achieve an efficient, professional, high-quality, market-ready unit turnover.

PRE-MOVEOUT WALK

14-30 days (about 4.5 weeks) prior to the resident moving out, there should be a pre-move-out walk and inspection completed to give your technicians an idea of what needs to be done. Carefully scour the unit, noting everything that needs to be done. **Note:** If there is a resident there that has a cleanliness issue and has not properly taken care of the unit, the appliances, or other objects in the unit, there should be another inspection done 24-48 hours (about 2 days) before the resident moves out.

Doing the pre-inspection here is what you will be looking for.

PLUMBING ISSUES / WATER LEAKS

Make sure the unit has no leaks. Turn on all water sources in the unit, kitchen and bathrooms. Make sure there are no leaks under kitchen and bathroom cabinets, and make sure there are no drips when faucets are off. Run the tub faucet and shower. Make sure the tub stem is functioning correctly and the shower head is not dripping, flush toilets to see if any leaks are present and check the toilet water supply line for rust or corrosion. When flushing the toilet, make sure there is no water pooling from under the toilet. After the toilet tank is filled, make sure the fill valve (this is the part that fills the toilet with water for flushing) is working correctly and shutting off when it reaches its desired level. Leaks can also come from appliances as well. If applicable, run the dishwasher and drain the water to make sure the dishwasher is accurately draining. Check the water supply coming from the dishwasher as well. Moving to the unit refrigerator water line, make sure the water line is snug to its fittings and there is no leak present. Also, make sure there are no kinks in the line. Most refrigerator water lines are made of thin copper that easily bends, so kinks can lead to a leak, especially if the fridge is being moved. Now you must check for ice build-up in the refrigerator's freezer section. Ice build-up can lead to water pooling at the bottom of the fridge, which can lead to drywall or flooring damage and needs to be attended to immediately. Remember to be thorough when checking for water leaks. Inspect ceilings and flooring for water damage or leaks. **Note:** In most cases, the discoloration can be a sign of water leaks or earlier water leaks. If discoloration is found and you are not sure if the damaged area has been repaired, be thorough and check with your property manager to make sure the area was repaired before being painted. Check window seals and windowpanes for discoloration or worn-out caulking and sealant. This can lead to leaks also.

ELECTRICAL ISSUES / LIGHTING FIXTURES

Ensure all light fixtures are installed and working correctly. To properly check all electrical issues the technician must have.

1. Gfci outlet tester.
2. Voltage tester.

Use the Gfci (Ground fault circuit interrupter) tester to make sure outlets and Gfci outlets are installed properly. For techs with minor experience in electrical, here is how your tester works. On the back of the Gfci tester will be a diagram to inform you what color combinations indicate correct and incorrect installations. Checking for any exposed wiring **Warning**: When exposed wiring is found, **do not touch wires**. Use your voltage meter to see if the wiring has voltage/power circulating through it. Place the tip of your tester to the exposed wire. You will hear a beeping sound or see a light blinking on your tester, depending on what type of tester you have. If power is circulating through the wire and you are certified to perform electrical duties in your city or state, carefully secure the wires and remove them out of the way for the security of others who will be in the unit doing the unit turn process. **Call a licensed electrician immediately if you are not certified by your city or state.**

PAINTING / DRYWALL REPAIRS

Thoroughly look over unit walls, ceilings, baseboards, and trim. If patchwork is needed, calculate how much wall compound is needed. If there are major drywall repairs, measure areas where drywall is needed and make a note of it. To get the correct amount of paint needed for the unit, measure the height of the wall in feet and inches and measure the width of the wall in feet and inches if there are any windows or doors measured from their edges to the opposite side of the wall multiply the height times the width and subtract windows and door openings measure in every room. This will give you the correct amount of paint needed for the unit.

WINDOWS / DOORS

If applicable, check window coverings and get a count of how many blinds the unit needs and the sizes of the blinds. Make sure there are no cracked or broken windows. Make sure all windows stay up when lifted and latch correctly and all window hardware and screens are present and not damaged. Be sure to check all doors entry, bedrooms, bathrooms, and closet doors (bifold, sliding, or accordion doors); all have the proper hardware to open and close properly and are not damaged.

FLOORS, SHELVES AND VENTILATION

Flooring: Hardwood/Laminate: Check for scratches, gaps, holes, loose floorboards, unlevel or protruding flooring, discoloration, or peeling polyurethane.

Ceramic / Porcelain / Marble flooring: Check for cracked, broken, loose tiles, unleveled or protruding tiles, and gaps in grout lines

Closet shelving / Kitchen cabinet shelving: Make sure all closet shelving is sturdy, has proper hardware present, and is installed correctly. Make sure all kitchen cabinets close properly, handles and hardware are present and not loose, and all shelving is present.

Heating Ventilation and Air Conditioning (HVAC): Make sure Batteries work in the thermostat. Make sure the heat/air conditioning is working correctly and filters are changed. Check all vents and ventilations for proper airflow. Remember to contact contractors for damage or missing parts if you are not licensed or certified to repair the issue yourself.

TRICKS OF THE TRADE

When painting a unit, using certain painting materials can assist you in getting the job done quickly.

1. 18-inch paint roller sleeve.

2. Hockey stick style paintbrush.

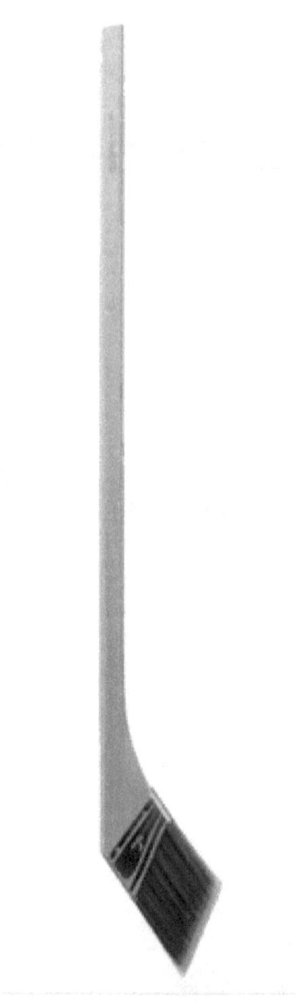

3. Hotdog Style Paint roller.

4. 14-inch paint roller sleeve.

5. Scotch-brite stainless steel scrubbing pad.

6. Painting /drywall stilts

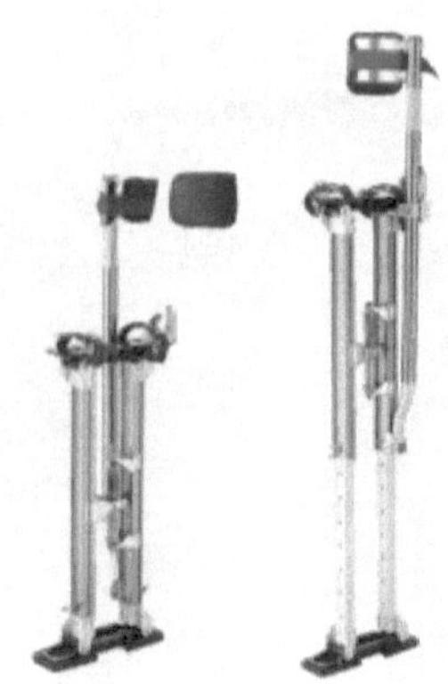

The 18/14-inch roller covers more space than the traditional roller. The hockey stick style Brush allows you to cut the walls without a ladder. The painting stilts are used for lofty ceilings without having to climb up and down a ladder. The hotdog style roller helps with hard-to-reach areas.

Painting tip: If the entire unit needs to be painted, instead of precise painting on the ceiling, the walls, and the baseboards and trim, use the 14 inch roller for the ceilings without cutting the ceiling. Place the roller at the corner of the ceiling touching. Don't care if the paint gets on the wall because you'll cut the wall last. This technique saves you a lot of time and can also be used for the walls.

Wall compound Tip: If there are small abrasions and holes in the wall, spackling wall compound cures more quickly than the average wall compound, but this works for small holes only.

Plumbing tip: When changing a bathroom or kitchen faucet and the water shut off valves are not working correctly with flexible compression lines, you can fold the line, use a pair of vice grips to hold the fold together, and proceed with changing the faucet.

Flooring: Instead of using a measuring tape, you can use a contour gauge when making flooring difficult.

Janitorial / Cleaning: Removing paint splatter can be quick and simple with warm soapy water and a Scotch-Brite stainless steel pad. This can be used on hardwood and vinyl floors, but not on ceramic, marble, or porcelain flooring. First, get a bucket of warm soapy water and a Scotch-Brite stainless steel pad. Dip the steel wool in the warm soapy water and light rub across the area that needs to be cleaned. Always go with the direction of the wood grain, otherwise the flooring may be damaged. This allows you to clean paint splatter a bit faster. Gather all the information needed to purchase materials and contact the correct contractors if necessary.

www.ingramcontent.com/pod-product-compliance
Lightning Source LLC
Chambersburg PA
CBHW020455180726
47992CB00026B/1431